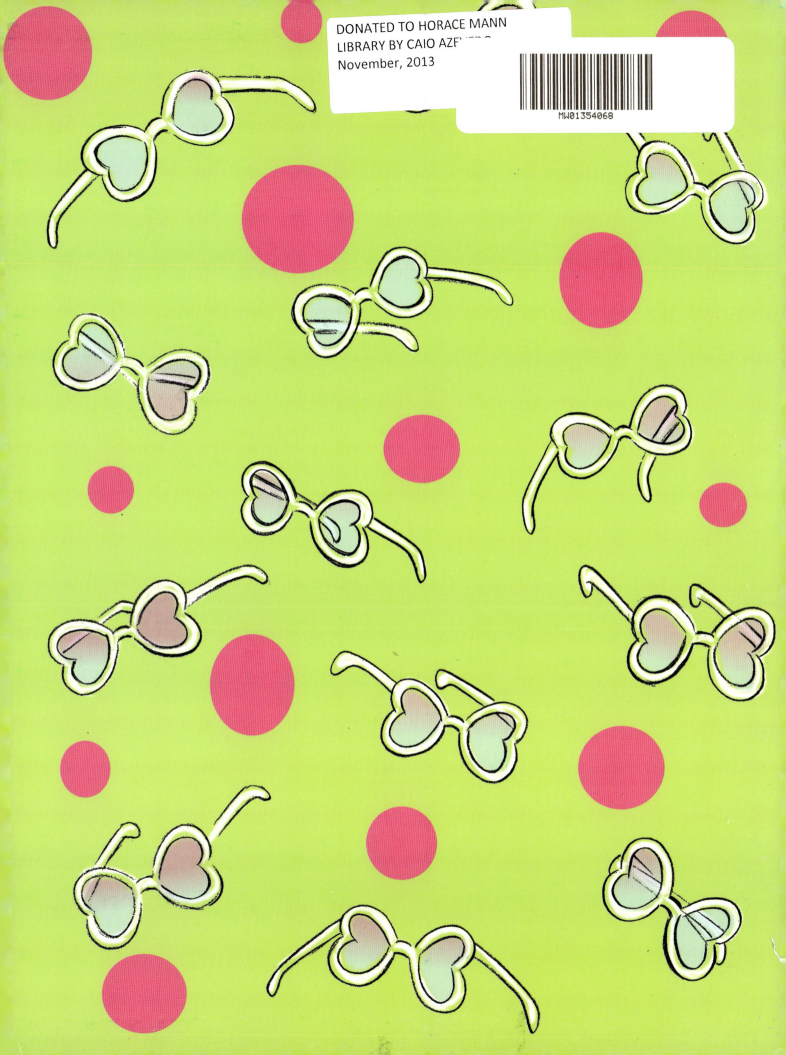

Tiny Hands Publishing, LLC

19 Shelter Cove Ln, Suite 207
Hilton Head Island, SC 29928

Text Copyright 2010 by Connie Sewell
Illustrations Copyright 2012 by Connie Sewell

Book Design by Erika Maston, Norsu Media
Edited by Emma D Dryden, Drydenbks

Published in 2013 by Tiny Hands Publishing, LLC

Library of Congress Cataloging-in-Publication Data available upon request

All rights reserved. No portion of this book may be reproduced in whole or part in any form, including electronically, photocopying, recording, or otherwise, without the written permission from the publisher or author.

Reviewers may use passages or text from the book for reviews only.

For information about bulk rate discounts, please contact Tiny Hands Publishing at info@tinyhandspublishing.com.

To contact the author for a book event, media and press, or live speaking, please email Connie Sewell at connie@summersaltz.com.

The text for this book is set in Crayon Crumble.
The illustrations for this book are rendered in pencil then colored digitally.

Printed in China.

For other fun activities and mechandise, please visit
www.summersaltz.com.

Book Summary: When Summer Saltz gets a new pair of ever-so-sassy white sunglasses, she takes on a personality all her own. But when she shows up for the party with her "I'm so HOLLYWOOD" attitude, she finds out she's not so HOLLYWOOD after all. She learns how to overcome conflict and what it is to be a good friend, as her best friend is especially kind to her.

ISBN 978-0-9888324-0-4

Summer Saltz

"I'm so HOLLYWOOD!"

Written By
Connie Sewell

Illustrations by
Elyse Whittaker-Paek

To my amazing dad, who never had the chance to see Summer in person and experience the love from his two beautiful grandchildren. We miss you dearly. You are forever in our hearts.

To my beautiful family for making my life so amazing. I am so blessed to spend every day in your shadows. Thank you for all your love and support as I live out my dreams.

C.S.

Tiny Hands Publishing, LLC
Hilton Head Island, SC USA

Horace Mann Library
Beverly Hills, CA

My name is Summer Saltz. My mom says she loves summertime and that's why she named me Summer. My dad says my name fits me to a tee. "Fits me to a tee?" I ask. My mom says that's a figure of speech and it means my name fits me perfectly. Well, I think what fits me perfectly is anything PINK.

I LOVE PINK!

And another thing that fits me to a tee are my new white sunglasses.

It all started with these white sunglasses...

Last week I was shopping with my mom and I found these sunglasses I just had to have. They were sort of a weird shape, but super sassy. As soon as I put them on, a lady at the counter said, "Wow, you look so HOLLYWOOD!"

Next, I found a purse—
a **PINK** cupcake purse! None of my friends had a purse like this! I was sure I was so HOLLYWOOD!

That evening, my parents were having a party with some of their friends. "This is the perfect time to show off my HOLLYWOOD sunglasses and my cupcake purse," I thought.

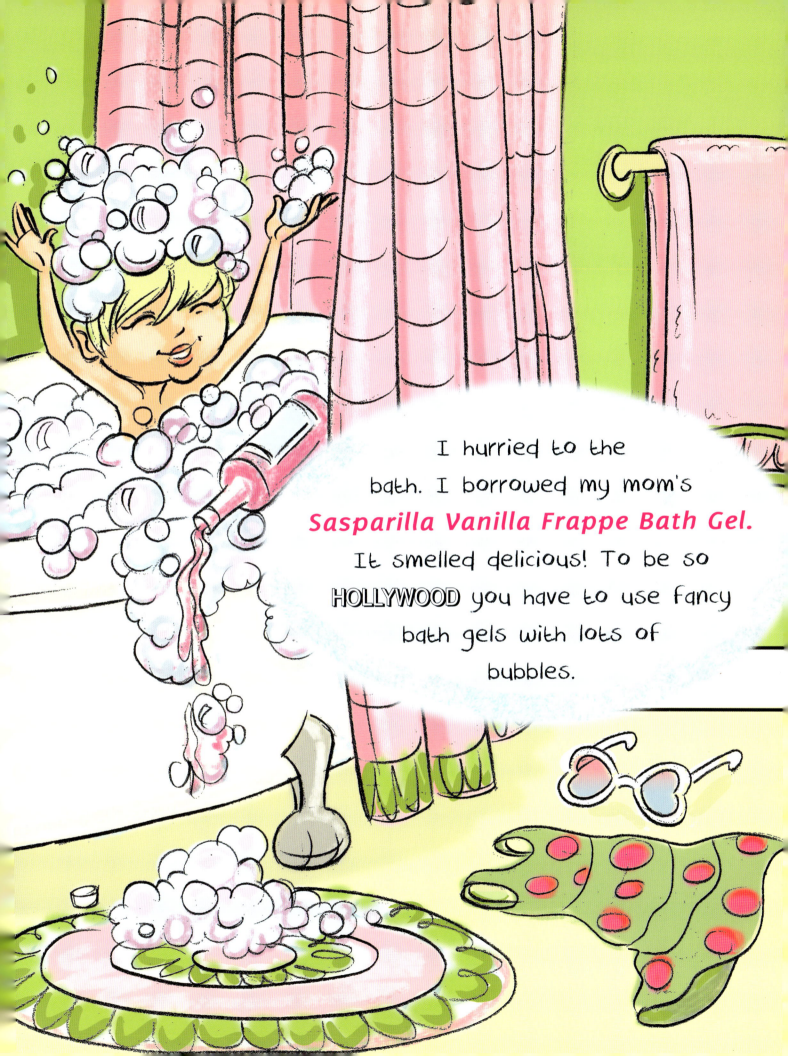

Next, I put on my favorite HOLLYWOOD outfit. Did I tell you that matching is most important if you want to be so HOLLYWOOD? Well, it is!

To be so HOLLYWOOD, you have to have a great hairstyle. My mom put my hair in ponytails with PINK glittery pompoms.

She made my eyes all sparkly and my cheeks a pretty PINK. Did I tell you?

I LOVE PINK!

It is always fun to have a friend at a party, so I decided to invite two: my dog Penelope and my best friend Molly. Penelope is BIG and clumsy, and she smells a little too, but I just love her! My dad says she's like a bull in a china shop. What does that even mean? Why would a bull be shopping in China?

Well anyway, my Aunt Jane says everyone in HOLLYWOOD carries their dogs in their purses.

How do you put a DOG in a purse?!

Later, my mom asked me to help her make food for her guests at the party. She says it's important to eat healthy. She says you should have all the food groups in your diet. She has a food chart and everything!

Well, I have my very own food chart too...

Finally, the doorbell rang. It was Molly...wearing the same exact HOLLYWOOD sunglasses! "How can this be," I thought, "I'm so HOLLYWOOD, not her!" I wanted Molly to just disappear!

POOF be gone! But she is my best friend.

"I like your sunglasses, Summer!" Molly said.

"I...um...like yours too, Molly. We are both so HOLLYWOOD!"

"What's so HOLLYWOOD?" Molly asked.

"You'll see! Come on! Let's go to the party!"

All of my parents' friends had arrived. It was time to make my grand entrance. Holding on to Penelope's collar, we made our way toward the kitchen. Molly followed behind. All of a sudden, Penelope smelled food...

"I'm not so HOLLYWOOD now!" I cried.

Molly stood there chewing her nails. She always chews her nails. She picked my sunglasses up off the floor. "I think you may need a new pair," she said softly.

Molly went home and I went up to my room. My mom came in later. "Let's talk about HOLLYWOOD, Summer," she said. "HOLLYWOOD is a place where movie stars and famous people live and work. It is not a personality or a way to describe you. When someone says 'You look so HOLLYWOOD,' that means you're stylish and fashionable. It's just a figure of speech."

I knew just what that meant!

She gave me a hug and a kiss. "We will try to fix your sunglasses tomorrow, Little Miss HOLLYWOOD."

The next day, Molly was playing on her skateboard and I was in my PINK car. "Thanks for coming to the party, Molly." I said.

"I'm sorry about your sunglasses, Summer. I have something for you." She pulled a pair of white sunglasses from her pocket. "You can have mine," she said.

"Climb in Molly, let's go for a ride! I hear everyone in HOLLYWOOD has a chauffeur. I'll be yours!"

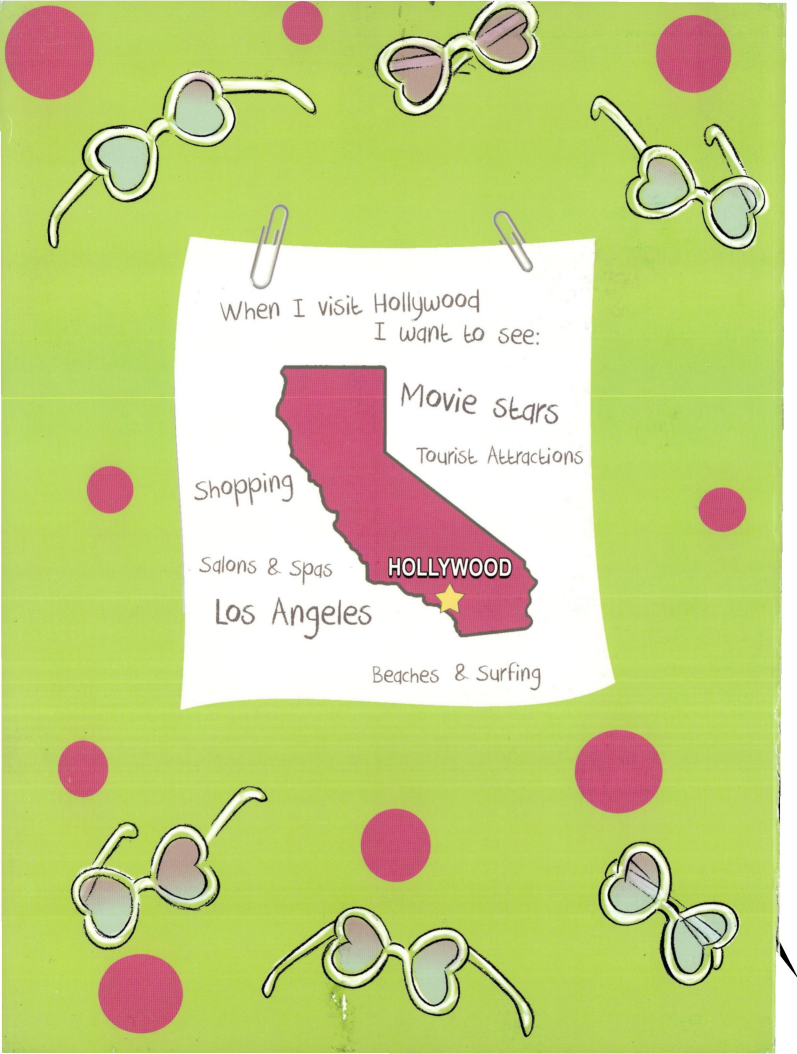